Lerner SPORTS

BEHIND THE SCENES
FOOTBALL

by James Monson

Lerner Publications ◆ Minn

D1472243

Lerner Publications Company
A division of Lerner Publishing Group, Inc.
241 First Avenue North
Minneapolis, MN 55401 USA

For reading levels and more information, look up this title at www.lernerbooks.com.

The images in this book are used with the permission of: © Maddie Meyer/Getty Images Sport/Getty Images, p. 1; © Nick Wosika/Icon Sportswire/Getty Images, pp. 4–5; © Mike Ehrmann/Getty Images Sport/Getty Images, p. 6; © JoeSAPhotos/Shutterstock.com, pp. 8–9, p. 11; © Tom Szczerbowski/Getty Images Sport/Getty Images, p. 13; © George Gojkovich/Getty Images Sport/Getty Images, pp. 14–15, 20–21; © David Maxwell/Getty Images Sport/Getty Images, pp. 16–17; © Bob Levey/Getty Images Sport/Getty Images, p. 19; © Michael Zagaris/San Francisco 49ers/Getty Images Sport/Getty Images, pp. 22–23; © Shareif Ziyadat/Getty Images Entertainment/Getty Images, pp. 24–25; © David Berding/Icon Sportswire/Getty Images, p. 26; © Amy Myers/Shutterstock.com, p. 29.

Front Cover: © Maddie Meyer/Getty Images Sport/Getty Images.

Main body text set in Myriad Pro.
Typeface provided by Adobe.

Library of Congress Cataloging-in-Publication Data

Names: Monson, James, 1994– author.
Title: Behind the scenes football / James Monson.
Description: Minneapolis : Lerner Publications, [2020] | Series: Inside the sport | Includes bibliographical references. | Audience: Age 7–11. | Audience: Grade 4 to 6.
Identifiers: LCCN 2018049358 (print) | LCCN 2018055007 (ebook) | ISBN 9781541556287 (eb pdf) | ISBN 9781541556058 (lb : alk. paper) | ISBN 9781541574366 (pb : alk. paper)
Subjects: LCSH: Football—Training—Juvenile literature. | Football players—Health and hygiene—Juvenile literature. | Football players—United States—Conduct of life—Juvenile literature. | Football players—United States—Charitable contributions—Juvenile literature. | National Football League—Juvenile literature.
Classification: LCC GV953.5 (ebook) | LCC GV953.5 .M66 2020 (print) | DDC 796.332/64—dc23

LC record available at https://lccn.loc.gov/2018049358

Manufactured in the United States of America
1-CG-7/15/19

CONTENTS

COMING UP
SHORT

There were only fifty-eight seconds left on the clock. Tom Brady and the New England Patriots trailed the Philadelphia Eagles 41–33 during Super Bowl LII. But the Patriots had been the most successful team in the National Football League (NFL) for years. Now they had one last shot. They just needed to go 91 yards down the field to score and tie the game. Brady quickly got to work.

The Patriots made it just short of midfield with nine seconds remaining. This was the last chance for Brady to throw a touchdown pass. New England lined up.

Quarterback Tom Brady passes the ball during Super Bowl LII. ▶

FACTS
at a Glance

- Many kids start playing tackle football at twelve or thirteen years old. Before that, they play flag football.

- Football players must be three years out of high school before entering the NFL Draft. Most players use that time to play college football.

- NFL players have to deal with a lot of media attention. After each game, players answer questions from reporters in the locker room.

- Many football players connect with fans through social media.

Brady got the ball and waited for his receivers to run all the way to the end zone.

Brady waited and waited. Then he finally threw the ball. It went high in the air. The ball came down near two Patriots receivers. But it hit the ground. The game was over. In that dramatic final stop, the Eagles had won their first Super Bowl.

Each Sunday during football season, players like Brady take the field and fans get to see their amazing skills. But being a professional football player is much more than just playing on Sundays. There are workouts, strict diets, and interactions with fans. It's a long path for players who want to be at the top of the NFL.

◄ **Tom Brady talks with his teammate James White during Super Bowl LII.**

CHAPTER 1

MAKING IT BIG

The path to the pros for many football players starts when they are about six or seven years old. Players used to start tackle football at this age. But today many start by playing flag football until they are about twelve or thirteen years old.

Many football players grow up playing multiple sports, such as basketball, baseball, or wrestling. If young players are good enough, colleges start recruiting them when they are sophomores or juniors in high school. Some are recruited even earlier. Dylan Moses was offered a scholarship by Louisiana State University in 2012. He was only entering eighth grade.

Young football players can play on school teams. ▶

He ended up playing at the University of Alabama.

College assistant coaches are usually the first ones to talk to players during recruitment. Then, if the college's head coach likes the player, he will meet with the player to decide whether to offer a scholarship. Recruiting websites rank high school players by ability. This can also help college coaches find players.

Once a football player enters college, he must stay there for three seasons before he is eligible for the NFL Draft. Scouts from NFL teams watch college games to see players the team might want to draft in the future.

The NFL Draft takes place each spring. The draft is seven rounds long. But many college players do not get drafted into the NFL.

Stats Spotlight
5

That's the record for most first overall picks from a single school. Both the University of Notre Dame and the University of Southern California (USC) have had that many players taken first. The last number one pick from USC was Carson Palmer, who was drafted by the Cincinnati Bengals in 2003.

High school football players do their best to attract the attention of college recruiters.

Those players can sign with a team as a free agent to try to earn a spot on a team. The players drafted in the first two or three rounds almost always make the roster of the teams that drafted them. They also might have a chance to be on the field right away. Others spend time as backups and try to improve their game in practice. However, most college players never play pro football.

There are no women playing in the NFL. There are some smaller leagues working to boost professional women's football. However, some women work in the NFL as coaches. Kathryn Smith joined the Buffalo Bills in 2016 as the first full-time female assistant coach in NFL history.

Kathryn Smith made history as the first female NFL assistant coach.

CHAPTER 2

ACTION ON
GAME DAY

NFL players are serious about game day. It starts with a good breakfast. The meal usually includes different foods such as oatmeal, meat, fruit, and vegetables. Players try to eat one big meal about four hours before the game starts. They avoid greasy foods like french fries. These unhealthful foods can slow down a football player.

After eating, players go to the locker room and start getting ready. Their pregame outfit is usually a T-shirt and shorts. Players will wear more if the game is in cold weather. During the warmup players run and stretch.

Antonio Brown of the Pittsburgh Steelers warms up before a game. ▶

Some try to ease the pain of bumps and bruises. Trainers make sure they all feel ready to play.

Once the game gets closer to starting, players put on all of their pads. They usually have pads for their legs and shoulders along with a helmet. Players also try to protect their knees and ankles with tape and braces. This helps prevent injuries by limiting how much those joints can move.

Players go onto the field in a full uniform to work on different parts of the team's game plan. They run practice plays, stretch more, and make sure they feel ready for the game. Then the teams go back to the locker room. When the game starts, the home team often comes out to dramatic music and screaming fans.

Players talk with coaches on the sidelines about how to beat their opponents.
▼

During the game, players work together on the field. They go through different plays to try to score touchdowns. Off the field, they talk with coaches and other players about how to beat their opponent.

At the end of most games, both teams run onto the field. The players tell each other "good game." The winning team's players will cheer and high-five each other. Teams celebrate even more during the playoffs. When a team wins the Super Bowl, the players all hug and cheer while lifting up the championship trophy.

The head coaches and star players talk in front of a large group of reporters after the game. The other players get interviewed at their lockers. They answer questions in front of TV cameras.

J. J. Watt of the Houston Texans speaks to a reporter.

Once they're done with the media, players often cool down in cold water to relax their muscles. They also refuel their bodies with a protein shake or a sandwich. Their next full meal doesn't come until hours after the game. They'll eat lean meats, fruits, and vegetables. Football players usually have an entire week to prepare for the next game.

CHAPTER 3

FOOTBALL NEVER SLEEPS

Football has become a year-round sport. Players are always worried about being in the best physical shape. During the season, players spend their weekdays working out to make sure they stay strong. On a normal week, when a team plays on Sunday, the players get Tuesday off to rest. They practice every other day. Players also practice during the off-season.

Football teams are always trying new things to help players feel their best. Players sit in hot or cold water to relax their muscles. They do different stretches to stay loose and avoid pulling their muscles. One new thing players are trying is cryotherapy.

Cole Beasley of the Dallas Cowboys stretches before a game. ▶

Adrian Colbert of the San Francisco 49ers studies videos to prepare for games. ▶

During cryotherapy, a player stands in a small room and turns as cold air hits him. People believe this helps get blood rushing through a person's body and keeps his muscles loose.

Players spend plenty of time studying videos of games. They watch their own games to see how they can get better. They also watch upcoming opponents' games so they know what to expect. Teams are always adjusting to what their opponents are doing.

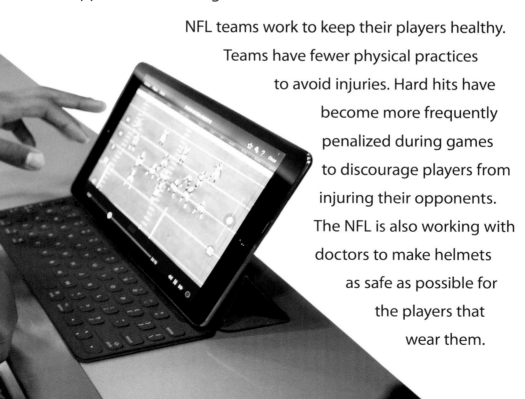

NFL teams work to keep their players healthy. Teams have fewer physical practices to avoid injuries. Hard hits have become more frequently penalized during games to discourage players from injuring their opponents. The NFL is also working with doctors to make helmets as safe as possible for the players that wear them.

CHAPTER 4

GIVING BACK

N FL players care about more than just football. Several players make headlines for positive things they do off the field.

Many players participate in charity events throughout the season. Cincinnati Bengals quarterback Andy Dalton raised $220,000 for families with seriously ill or disabled children at an event in 2018. Other players have started their own charity organizations. Philadelphia Eagles quarterback Carson Wentz's AO1 Foundation has a food truck in Philadelphia that gives out food to those in need.

New York Giants quarterback Eli Manning participates in a charity event for the Hank's Yanks organization to support youth baseball and community service projects. ▶

Players such as Kirk Cousins of the Minnesota Vikings use social media to connect with their fans.

Players also like to connect with fans off the field. Many do this through social media. Fans have a chance to see what life is like for players through Instagram, Twitter, or Facebook. Some players post videos of their workouts or vacations. Others post about their families. Minnesota Vikings quarterback Kirk Cousins posted a photo on his social media in 2018 announcing that he and his wife were expecting their second child.

With a focus on player safety, the sport of football continues to change. The league is working to find new ways to help players stay safe and healthy. Still, even as some things change, the NFL continues to keep millions of fans on the edge of their seats.

YOUR TURN

Star quarterbacks have to learn how to throw the ball short and far. Players like Tom Brady have to throw the ball to wide receivers that can be close by or way down the field. This pass and catch drill is a perfect way for young players to work on being a better passer.

This drill needs at least two people, but there can be more than that. First, make groups of two. Make sure one player has a football. Then, each pair should be about five yards apart. The player with the ball starts by throwing it to their partner. Do this back and forth a few times to get warmed up.

After a few throws, it's time to have some fun. One player throws a pass to her partner. If he catches it, the team is in the game. If the pass is dropped, the pair is out and sits down until the game is over. Whenever a player catches a pass, both partners take a step back. The pairs continue playing catch until there is just one pair remaining.

Young football players must practice catches and other basic skills.

In the end, players will get to try throwing passes at different distances while having some fun together!

GLOSSARY

charity
related to an organization that raises money for a certain cause

end zone
the part of a football field where a team has to go to score a touchdown

game plan
a plan for a team to beat its opponent in a game

greasy
covered with oil and usually high in fat

interviewed
to be asked questions

recruiting
trying to get a player to join a certain team

refuel
to get back energy after doing a lot of work

scholarship
money provided to a person to pay for their college because of the person's skill in a sport or in school

trainers
employees of a football team who help players with injuries and help them get stronger

warmup
stretching or practice done in preparation for an athletic event

FURTHER INFORMATION

Editors of Sports Illustrated Kids. *The Greatest Football Teams of All Time.* New York: Time Inc. Books, 2018.

Gramling, Gary. *The Football Fanbook.* New York: Liberty Street, an imprint of Time Inc. Books, 2017.

Morey, Allan. *Football Records.* Minneapolis: Bellwether Media, Inc., 2018.

National Football League
http://www.nfl.com

Pro Football Hall of Fame
http://profootballhof.com

Savage, Jeff. *Football Super Stats.* Minneapolis: Lerner, 2018.

INDEX

ABOUT THE AUTHOR

James Monson is a sportswriter based in the Minneapolis-Saint Paul area. He has written articles that have appeared in various publications across the country. He has a degree in print/digital sports journalism.